Tao Of Blackness

Volume Two

By

H.E. EDWARDS

Table of Contents

In Loving Memory

In loving memory to a dear close friend Sam Mayo who always supported my poetry with love and encouragement to whom I never got the chance to say thank you or goodbye .This book is dedicated in his memory and spirit of a man whom all knew will never be forgotten.

We shall never forget all that was all lost to keep those
memories alive
-H.E.Ewards

Acknowledgements

This book is dedicated to all of my sons whom I love deeply and hope they understand being aware of the world they live in and the society that they belong to. This book is for them to understand who I was and became like a man and hopefully, they will pass it along to their next generation the same way I'm passing it along to them, with love. This book is not only for my sons, but it is also for your sons and daughters as well.

For: Arien,

Jalen, Harold, Tremayne, and Kendall

Twitter: @heedwardspoetry

Instagram: @heedwardspoetry1

Email: heedwards100@gmail.com

About The Book

Tao of Blackness 2 is the second volume of poetry by poet H.E.Edwards that picks up where he le off from volume one. It is a bold and riveting collection of poems that capture the mentality of an African American man living in this country through his own perception. Tao of Blackness volume two makes you take a closer look at where we been in this country and how far we have to go to change our views on how we see each other as God's children. Volume One was written by his younger self over 20 years ago and volume 2 is a collection of poems by an older more socially conscious version of the author. This book is a mirror for some people and a legacy for others that need to understand what lies on the other side of the tracks. This book is also for future generations to understand the times we are living and what kind of times we choose to go in another positive direction.

Introduction By Katie Moran

Tao of Blackness Volume 2 is a must read for our time by author and poetry realist H.E. Edwards speaks an urgent message for our nation on upholding the ideals of Justice, Equality, and Freedom. A 21st Century poet, H.E. Edwards calls for the strength and dignity of Blackness to revolutionize our time, to make a better world and to recognize the dignity and worth in every human being. Tao of Blackness Volume 2 acknowledges the American disavowal of Blackness, racial injustice, and unjust systemic racism in the everyday life of Black men. With power and righteous anger, H.E. Edwards is a voice for justice in our world. His passionate and kind-hearted spirit shines through his work and li s our nation to a higher standard, as he de-mands the just realization of the rights of all people. I am honored to be a part of this work and to call him a friend.

Katie Moran is the CEO & Founder of Thetis & Themis Inclusive Equanimity and author of the Periwinkle Wishes

Instagram: @thekatiemoran

Twitter: @katieemorann

"If you're not careful, the media will have you hating the people who are being oppressed, and loving the people who are doing the oppressing".

-Malcolm X

BLACKOUT

blackout

they told me
that
I wasn't good enough
they told me
that
I wasn't talented enough
they told me
that
I wasn't determined enough
and then they had the nerve to tell me
that
I wasn't black enough
I came into the room, and look
around at all who was there
and begin
to smile, because
I knew deep down within me
I was ENOUGH of
everything they thought I wasn't

put on notice

we are not
all the same........white people
we
don't all look alike
caus' I don't know Pookie or
never ever knew anybody named JOJO
so
I hope you now know

WE DON'T EAT PORK OR
EAT ALL OF OUR FOOD FRIED
AND HANG OUT DOWN AT THE CORNER
JUST HAVING A GOOD OLE TIME

because most of us have more
important things to do

we are not all dropouts, or
thuggish hood rats
that love to hustle all day
and Rap Rap Rap

we certainly all are not
DEMOCRATS
in outdated suits.....just
waiting around just to vote for
the next great white hope
NOPE!!!

we are not the equivalent
of poor white trash
livin' in a hopeless bliss

we are a special unique kind of
PEOPLE
and I hope you all would
just understand

death sentence

the meek and innocent
will suf er
at the hands of the so-called
righteous ones
who fear no God
AMERICA becomes the
home of death
and psychotic rage
full of bloodthirsty people
who's hypocrisy, has no bounds

your president even admits it
"I will force the past upon you, whether
you like it or not"
and for those who dream for a better
WAY OF LIFE
will be cast into their sea of fire

the INJUSTICES
haunts America from the ghosts
of it's past
and as we live for a
change to fall upon us
we become more
disillusioned
by their fate

revolution review

every Revolution
starts
and ends with bloodshed

it comes with
dedication and
it comes without fear
then dies
a slow and agonizing death

as we have to rise up
to be counted not as casualties
but as people of change

in the annals of the mind
it becomes a reckless obsession,
to want what they refuse to give you
and then that recklessness
dies a slow death

we become defiant
as our dreams dissipate
into a review of our past

crash

days
fall upon me
like wet leaves from
a rotted tree
it becomes a sign
of change
that
I'm unfamiliar with
the scars from my body
reflect
my true identity
and so
I become the image of
your hate

black sheep

I become that man
not a negro
not a colored
not a black man
not African-American
or not even a nigger!
but
a man
a breathing human being
a child of God
livin' on the edge
of a tragic history that is
not just yours, but
also mine
I am the shattered image
of peace among all
mankind
neglected and torn
between two worlds that
I don't fit in
but I matter and you can't tell me
that I don't!
I dream
but, you can't tell me that
it's not real
I belong
and you can't tell me that
I don't!

show of force

they came with their vengeance
with rage upon us
abusing their authority
against those that are labeled
the unjust
their sirens are loud but
not as aggressive as their
force
they came, not with honor
but with violence
raining down upon the
very people, they were sworn to protect
black people brown people
we will lift each other from the ashes
and residue
from our fallen ones
and
when we can't breathe,
let our cries be heard around
the world
Saying, let us up!!!

uneasy grave

Malcolm X shot down in a hail of bullets
too young to die, so much left undone
he was taken too soon, a void left
in the soul of Black America

Martin Luther King Jr shot by
an assassin's bullet before his prime
he was taken too soon, died too young
so much left undone, a tragedy in the
hearts of Black America

Medgar Edgers shot and killed
by a man with rage, he died too soon
so much undone, he could have been the one
but became the spirit of Black America

the fallen men of the movement are dead
but their graves are unrestful at peace
because we are still fighting for a democracy
not just for some, but for all
and hate took them all away

every man

every man
should not believe that
life for him is better
not until he is treated equal
he should fight for change in every way
and never stop until his dying day

he should pass it along to the young
and teach them well
so, when the days go by into years
only time will tell

every man
should look into his heart
and the depths of his soul
teach it to your young
to be passed on down from the old

respect your women, like queens
and rare jewels
look at her beauty like a painted
murals

think out loud and love yourself,
because if you don't then
it becomes of nobody else

madness

I am the voice of resistance
the calm of humanity

a silhouette of a dream
of what it could have been

the lover of justice
torn between dif erent kinds of people
colliding against righteousness

I become the bearer of
Truth

as Hope becomes shrouded into
a dark abliss

I am that man, a living image
in a world gone mad

justice for Breonna

I never been to Louisville Kentucky but
I felt her spirit overwhelm my heart
overtaking my inner being

I say her name.....it is.
'Breonna Taylor'
I say it loud with truth and meaning
because she mattered

no justice for her today and
maybe not tomorrow either
when they victimized her rights
and violated her home on that
fateful tragic night

I say her name.....with love
'Breonna Taylor'
because she mattered to me
long before she was murdered by the police

no justice for her tomorrow
or maybe sometime never but
we'll keep on saying her name
Breonna Taylor so they shall never forget
because she rally did mattered
not just for some, but for all

ABSENCE OF THE HEART

love casualty

the mating season called
and my manhood peaks
in fool bloom
so when a woman finds you
a little bit fancy
then what is a man to do?

love has her soul at your will
divine on her every touch
and these are the simplest things
a woman craves so much

for when love comes
suddenly
a slithered tongue lies
then heartache and pain begins thereafter
when a shivering heart has died

love her or
leave her
then, maybe set her free
as she becomes just another victim of
a love casualty

i came

I came
like bonfires insanity
being just like one of
the guys
I loved so many women
and told a few lies

I dreamed
but never too fast
and held on to foolish
trends
that had came
and long have passed

I lived
like an endless sunset
but faded, like a cool breeze
on a Summers day
I may have stayed a little bit too long
and then drifted slowly away

she's leavin' today

she says she's leavin' today
taking the car kids and the dog away
because life with me just isn't the same
and she feels like nothin's
ever gonna change

she's leavin' today, not
wanting to wait till tomorrow
and she says that if she stays
any longer
it would add to her many sorrows

well there isn't much I can tell her
to make her change her mind
and if we continue to argue and
fight
it really would be a waste of our lives

so I'll let her take the car kids and even
the dog
if she wants to free
because life would surely be good
for us both
being unmarried but happy

born not to know

it is said that, money
can't buy you love
but
it can buy you a little bit
of respect

it is said that, money
is the root of all evil,
but
I never even found that tree

it is said that
you reap
what you sow, but
nothin' good has ever came
from my pain

and there were some things
I was born not to know

black

BLACK
is
the new color
of Triumph
and Prosperity

BLACK
is
the new definition of
Hope and Change

BLACK
is
the new symbol of
Peace Unity and Divine
Wisdom

BLACK
is
the new foundation
to build it all on

BLACK
is
the new thing called
LOVE

the cure

there is no cure
for what ails you, so I guess
you must have been born that way
no cure for your ignorance and
ungodly ways
not loving your fellow child of
God
I weep for you, born to only
love yourself and others who share
your views
there is no cure for living a lie
you created, just to keep what
you got
no vaccine cures racism
it certainly doesn't cure all the hatred
that you hold inside

the savages

black people
will never rise above him
all the scheming and the lies
they will never move any closer
to freedom
unless they all have died
back in the past, Master owned
your soul
he could rape, kill and maim you
then bury you deep in a hole
lynched before the sun went down
better get on home before
they run you out of town
black people
will never outsmart him
because he hates defeat
and he'll do whatever it takes to get ahead
even if he has to cheat

justice for all

oh say can you see
only far as freedom and equality
could be
what so proudly they held
was nothing they had of their own
and the only proof there was
kidnap rape torture and deceit and
robbery of humanity
the crackin' whips were heard
around the world
unjustly an act of bloodshed
as modern-day slavery would become to be
in a so-called world of democracy
that so many seemed to proud of

sometimes

sometimes I think
they
don't want to love
sometimes I think
they
choose not to know
sometimes I think
they
could never love anyone
else
who is not like their own
sometimes I think
they
would rather die
than embrace peace

more love

maybe soon, I mean like
really soon

I believe we are gonna have to rely on
just real love,
I mean true unconditional love
to survive
the kind of LoVe that keeps hope alive
and that kind of LoVe gives everybody all around
you
some kinda Peace of Mind

and with me...... that'll be just fine

we should only give LoVe
more than HATE
because good things come
if we just refuse to wait

give us more LoVe than politics
more LoVe than police,
even more LoVe than you"ll ever know
"so now just think about that for just a minute"
and then let all of your LoVe flow

we need more LoVe, you know
like the kind that never goes out of style
and then whenever we all get together
with all that LoVe we share,
it would definitely make
the whole world SMILE

TAKE A MESSAGE

take a message

take a message
to your **Mayor**
and tell him what he needs to know
too many of his policemen are out
on the streets
and some of them are
way out of control

take a message
to your **Governor**
and I hope we can make him see
that, what good is our neighborhood and
city
if we all dying from that dreaded disease

take a message
to your **Congressman**
and let him know just how you feel
and if he can't do the job you gave to him
then some other person will

take this message
directly
to your **President**
because he is openly blatantly
corrupt
and if he can't do his job for the
people who put him there
then you tell him his time is up

i used to be black, but now i'm just mad

I used to black, but now just I'm mad
as hell
just too many of my brothas'
and sistas' incarcerated and
sitting up in jail
don't have a reason why this must be
but I guess this is what is accepted in
our society

I used to be black, but now I am really mad
because we are never given our just due
and it would be really funny,
if wasn't so damn sad

I used to black, but now i'm just mad
at the system
tryin' to keep my people down
over 400 years of oppression
and them folks
still haven't come around

i used to be black, til i'm blue
but just plain mad at the
whole wide world and
what is a black man to do?

voter's rights

Mr. politician,
you can't buy me
because I got a voter's rights
and my vote isn't for free

you can't tell me what I want
and what I need to do
so take your lying ass back to Washington
in those shiny winged -tipped shoes

you talk a real good game
but it all sounds the same
tellin' me what I want to hear
and that's a doggone shame

Mr. Politician
why are you so hard to find
can't seem to know where you are
until it's around election time

promises, promises is what
got you elected
but ever since you've been on the job
all of your people feel neglected

repetition

lynchings
from a tree
we protest and march on
this is the way it must be
get yourself murdered in the deep dark South
let's protest and march on

can't sit in the front of
the bus
even though I have money in my hand
so, were gonna boycott protest
and march on

can't drink from this water fountain
no matter how thirsty I am
let's protest and march on
to a freedom song
haunting the air

Jim Crow is just plain outta control
let's protest and march
and we hope this will save their souls
so, let's keep on protesting and marching on

somebody killed those 4 little girls
in our church
we better get up and protest
and march on

then our king had fallen down
to an assassin's bullet
we have to go protest and march on
but, we still have a little time to
tear up this whole damn town

60 years ago and now
still catching hell worse than before

so, we gonna get up again to protest
and march
as the drama continues to unfold
on and on and on

no room for error

I am in an elevator
with an older white woman
she clinches her purse
and I hold my
breath

she nonchalantly glances at me
from the corner of her eye but
not in fear but
in anticipation

5 more floors to go
before she gets
of in a sighed relief
and doesn't have to see my face
ever again

take a bold dark look
around you lady
I am still the bad guy
in your eyes
even
after over 400 years in captivity
and being victimized
as the last class citizen
for over two centuries

and the only thing she is worried about
is her purse

let's take a ride

let's take a ride
down down down down memory
lane
let's take that journey into
that happy place

not way back in time
but right there within your mind
where nobody here knows
your name and
and there is no one color
because we are all the same

let's take a walk down
Lenox Avenue
which is now rightfully renamed
Malcolm X Blvd
because that brother
changed the game

let's stroll down by that street called
'I can't breathe"
which should be named in his honor
and I hope they get hip to that
if you know what I mean

I never want to have to call the police
but if I did
let's just pray to God
that they don't show
caus' that's just the way
it is
cruisin' down the street
of hope

take a closer look

I am what you come
to despise
so take a closer look
into these cold dark eyes

no fear
take a real good look at my face
because I'm still standing
right here

letting you get a full view
of what you can't control
and were becoming more defiant
from the young to
the old

take a real closer look
all around this country and
tell me what you see

millions upon millions of people
UN-restrained
just like me

never naive

I can not make you
LOVE me
but
I want to be free

I can not make you
TRUST me
but I want to be
free

I can not make you
RESPECT me
but I want to be free

free from a CRIME I did
Not commit
because that was you
not me

I can not make you
FEEL something that
you will never understand
even if the skies of heaven opened up
and the angels came out
to dance

I can not make you
care about me
because it is not in your heart
to want for me, what you would want for yourself

but at least I can tell you
what I really want
and that is, I just want to be
free

what i used to be

I am much older but more
wiser
deeper
but stronger
and peaceful in a militant
kinda way
make room for me
because I coming through
more aware
than I ever been
and when I arrive, they will
know I came
even though, I am no longer filled
with youth
but my vigor is what
helps me, to see my way through

their dreams become mine

their DREAMS
become mine
like father like the sons

they become what I couldn't be
full of life
unlimited hopes
ambitions and
a whole lot of DREAMS

my love for them runs
deep as a well
with their
creative minds and hustlin'
game

I know they'll be safe
in this world filled with love
and hate
I just know in my heart that
they will be
ok

NO NIGGERS HERE

no niggers here

NO niggers,
allowed UP in here!
but, **NIGGAS** are welcome to come
just the way they are
anytime they feel

dark-skinned- mulattoes
mocha colored Afro-Americaaaaaan
love them all the same,
every woman, child, and man

I never met a nigger
but, there's been a lotta'
real cool ass **NIGGAS** I know
and they are not too fond of that
other word, you dig?
just in case you didn't know

I never even seen just one nigger
in my whole entire life
but if, you call my **NIGGA**
a nigger
then you better' be ready to fight

black is black

Black is **Black**
and you can't take it back
from where YOU came
so my brothers and sisters
it's a family af air, so
we are all just the same

let me pick you up
if you should ever fall
to the ground
because as long as we share
so much in common
there we will always be
plenty enough of love to go around

Black is **Black**
I won't let you fall
through the crack
because as long as we are
all united so strong
we will always have each other's back

unrestrained

UNRESTRAINED
from
the bondage
i

never wanted
unconnected
from
what
once was and still is
I can say what I want
without feeling any guilt
and now I am just an

UNRESTRAINED
making it real
you want me to apologize for
something I never did
you were never held in captivity
by people of color

so what in the hell, is wrong with you?
I feel you breathing down my neck
every day I live
but I will never
forgive
or let go of this pain

no apologies

I can never and
won't
apologize for something
you did to me
never will I surrender and
falsify a dream
I won't apologize for living
your LIE
and if you are expecting an apology, then
you will be waiting
a long long time.
my people were brought against their will
never gave them a choice
to be slaves and be mistreated
I say NO.........no apologies here
I didn't invent the Jim Crow laws
nor did I ever agreed to be "Separate but Equal"
I did not choose to eat my food
in the back of the restaurant
parking lot
while you giving me the impression
that I'm not fit to eat
in the same room as you
I will NOT apologize, for how
you make me feel
or even more so
how I make me feel

not for sale

pride
it's not
for sale
my
self-respect
it's
not for sale
integrity
is mine
and it's definitely
not for sale

stand

Malcolm said it best
that
if you stand for nothing
then you will fall for
anything
and the man's words
ring true today
so stand
for something
if you want to be free
from tyranny
and hypocrisy
stand for
people that can't stand for themselves
stand
for what you truly believe
just stand up for
what they say you can't

freedom is near

freedom
is near
can you touch it?
it's all in the air, everywhere
like a cool breeze blowin'
can you feel it?
freedom
if you want it, you
can have it.....but
you must be willing to die
to keep it
and you certainly must be ready
to hold on to it and
never let it go
it is a gift from God and it
came without a receipt
and no,
you are not allowed to exchange it
or return it from where it came.
freedom is near
but, it can't be sold, bought
or given away
because it is the only valuable thing
you will ever own

revolution

talkin' about a
revolution
one that even disillusioned
minds
couldn't even comprehend
and if I remained silent any longer
I may begin to EXPLODE!!
I'm talkin' about a real
Revolution
coming like a freight train
running over everything in sight
every man woman and child of
Color
knows it's coming
just ask yourself, is it worth it?
or do you really want to go there
talkin' bout a revolution
even revolutionist couldn't visualize it
it becomes what every racist conservative
Fears
and it is a Reality

in the eyes of my people

in the eyes of my people
I see pain
I see what has been done to
their hearts and minds
in a country that no longer wants them
I see no love
only distrust from the scars
on their bodies and battered
souls
in the eyes of my people
they remain hopeful in a
hopeless world
seeking out what is theirs to own

psychological warfare

I do not FEAR you
never did....never will
I am the epitome of
Strength Determination and
Power
you can't control me
even if
you have me prosecuted and
locked away
I now know the Truth
and it is,
"you are no better than me"
never was....never will be
my mind is intelligently sound
and my heart beats like a
young lion roaring
you can never stop what
you never created
never have..... never did

the struggle continues

the struggle continues even after over 400 year later
oppression racism and all the obstacles put
forth against us
so we fight, not just for yourself but
for all of those that come after you
and even die if that's what it down comes to

there is no peace without justice and
no calmness without the rage within us
so fight and keep fighting for TRUTH
HOPE and RIGHTEOUSNESS
even if takes a whole lifetime,
because the struggle never ends, it continues

without KNOWLEDGE you will never understand
or see through the lies being told
and never rise above yourself
because living in these times is a struggle,
its a tragedy

POET IN A RAGE

poet in a rage

I can be dangerous, if
I have to be
but, isn't this what you all
expected from me?

I can go completely, ballistic
be a menace on this earth,
because I was born in a fit of rage
at the time of my birth

so what cage,
have you been locked up in
to be my foe instead of
a friend?

society sometimes makes me wish that
I was sometimes dead
sit down in a quiet place, and
put a gun to my head

but then I get on my knees
and start to pray
then wake up the next morning
to a very lovely day

what gives you all the right to
persecute me
when my mind and soul just
wants to be free

no one can judge me
but the good Lord up above
so, I hope you all just die,
and then return back to earth as
creatures of love

ego trippin'

I'm not a scholar, but
I feel like a king on
a make-believe throne
searching and roaming for my
queen t
call my own

I'm not a movie star
but, I shine like the moon at night
beaming of a plane on a runway
about to take flight

no, I'm not anything special
I'm just a simple plain man
with one hell of an ego trip
caught up near and far
somewhere in and between
in my dreams

death has no name

Death
shall have no name
for it cheats and schemes
to achieve it's wealth and
fame
Death really doesn't give
a damn who you are
you could be a famous athlete entertainer
politician
or a movie star
Death doesn't really care
who the hell you are when he's coming after you
and it really doesn't,t matter if
you had a lot more things to do
it has horrible timing
and travels to come and get you
near or far
and it certainly doesn't give a fuck
to know who the hell you are

bulletproof

I am lean,
my wingspan is long
I have a mind that is very complexed
and a heart that is so strong

so, shoot me stab me
if you will
but, you would be so disappointed in a man
that you can't even kill

I am a realist revolutionist extreme
opportunistic freak
birth and raised by a single black
mother
who has never know defeat

I am a hero to some women children
and men
and a bastard to a few who tried
to kill me again
some came after me again

and many have failed some even tried
but I slowly browed them away with my intelligence
and wit

so, they all mentally died
I am here today and will
be here tomorrow
to inflict more pain upon all your sorrows

psycho city rage

all of the city is
in a rage and those
innercity blues has got my mind
in a haze
and this is a crazy place that
I rather not be
so, would you mind locking me up
and throwing away the key

beggers and hustlers on every corner
just looking to make a dollar
but this psycho city rage in me
just makes you wanna holler

I'd like to drive away from here
and go somewhere real far
but gas is so damn expensive now,
that I have to leave my car

I want to! oh but, I need to!
gotta get away real soon
take the next Nasa shuttle flight and
head straight for the moon

too many people
in this overcrowded place
and if you blinked your eyes just once again
your liable to lose your space

the roads here are so bumpy
and the freeways are all just packed
too much weight for this little monkey
of mine
sitting on my back

hookers on every block
just looking to make some time
and my telephone keeps on ringing

and I'm about to lose my mind
I need to! oh, I just have to!
just find some way to leave
before this psycho city rage
in me
takes all of my mentality

not for sale

Pride
not for sale
my self-respect?
then you can really go to hell!!!!!
integrity
you can't have that neither
and my time
is so valuable that
nor can you have that either

when all the love in the world dies

what shall become of us
when the whole world stops loving,
and we never show any compassion
any remorse
do we stop living, and stop caring
for one another?
what becomes of our faith in
humanity
as we as human beings
cease to exist?
will be become like George Floyd and
stop breathing because there is no compassion,
or do those who murdered Breonna Taylor
have to pay for their ungodly sins?
when did the world stop loving and caring for
their fellow child of God?
"I wish I knew"
so, when all of the love in the world dies
do we die right along with it,
trying so hard to understand
the tragic side of life

5 to 9

hands and feet so weary
working back to back shifts
in the dawn of the night
and the stale stench of this thin air
sours my taste for life
as the rains came and quenched a
thirst I could no longer bare

I've showered in sunrays, sometimes
even on the coldest days
while my 2 am thoughts seem to flutter
away into thin air

cars drive by me on these dark and
lonesome streets
as I sit in my chairs looking out the
window of hope

the times

freedom-loving' people
all on the scene, bathing in
a sea of democracy
livin' in the times and being
behind in the times
and that becomes the story
we write for our children
but there shall be no peace until
we all have justice
not just justice for some
but all
we are livin' in these days
where love becomes a victim
of our own color
and no one is blind to the unjustly

all around us

civil rights were the ploy
of everything around us
and to this day, it still is,
for people of color trying
to figure out the Hate
and why we still have to always
show them that we exist
it becomes a dream, but it
soon faded away
until one man died that day
when he fatally said,
"I Can't Breathe"
he called out for his momma, and
she never came, but
the rest of us did
we heard his cries and his lost
dreams
he awakened the whole world with
a beautiful tragedy
and we begin to start a change
for progress that will never
end

BLACK EVOLUTION

black evolution

we become like a black
Evolution
to be a people of color
and race
all balled up in an emotional
rage
of what we are becoming
so used to

let's Evolve, but remain calm
life is our shuttle
to a great path
to our own fate
you can, if you want to,
Dream Out Loud
and never surrender the pain
because
this is what drives us al

caus' I am black

Arrested and
prosecuted faster than
the speed of light
caus' I am Black
and that's all they needed to know

Shot..... by the crooked police,
while minding
my own damn business!
caus' I am Black
and that's good enough of a reason
for them to kill me

Profiled
because I fit that description
and I am Black
so now, do you catch my drift?
let time change, let freedom ring
so when it is my time
I hope they let me
Sing

7 days

Monday is the day
that I start of my week
so when Tuesday gets here
I'm already dead on my feet
Wednesday will come soon
as the weekend is near
can hardly wait another minute
until Thursday is here
Friday I'm weary,
I need time to rest, but
it already seems like this was
the hardest week yet
Sunday I worship and take
time to pray
because I'm gonna need every bit of
God's help
just to make it through another weekday
Monday is here
another week is about to begin
and that's when I have to start
all of this madness all over again

black people

BLACK people
wake up!

BLACK people
stand up!
let them know that
we will suffer no more

BLACK people
rise up!

BLACK people
get riled up!!
and tell them what you are
asking for

this is that time
for us to shine,
and that moment
is **NOW!**

living in the city

living in the city
my mind and body grow quite
weary
from the heat blazing in the summertime
and the tensions run a little bit high

urban life is contagious
like a sweeping epidemic
floundering along the streetside curb
and become a part of my human
characteristics
I am confined, but not unwilling to a social
change
never content on being part of an unlikely
assimilation

I roam the streets,
in the very core of the city
in search of peace of mind and
and the rest is sunshine, even on a rainy day

living in the city, sometimes
is a tragedy
living day to day on a prayer
I live in the ghetto because I
live for the ghetto and it's
now a part of me

vision

a vision of a
blaze
that
ceased
to amaze
a glory of
abundance
in a world
that's way behind
the times
but, never more of
a door
that seems to
lead nowhere that
we wanted to go
the truth
seems to be
no more but
lies
and integrity and pride
is all we know
we become in search
of
a light in the
dark
hoping to find
that there is nothing
there but empty hopes
and false
Dreams

unspoken truth

we must
come together
we must
learn the truth
we must follow that path
and we must conquer it
with love
we must become one
like Gemini's at birth
let go of the pain
that is within the depths of our
hearts and minds
we must
denounce the past
because there is no honor
in a history
that reak of blood
from tortured souls
we must
show a higher love to those
that are willing to give it so freely
let us fight if we must
but bare no regrets if
death comes

refuge

I seek shelter from
their rage
I seek
some kind of understanding
from their ignorance
I seek a path for
righteousness and
even if I must Die
so it shall be
I seek Truth from
their lies
told long stories ago
when people of color were
kidnaped from their native homeland
I seek love
if they are willing to give it
and I will be happy to pass it along
I seek protection from
laws that are supposed to
give me a sense of
security
and I seek out a justice
that is fit for a
King

Color

this COLOR
defines me,
but
it's not even close to
WHO I Am
as a person
not just as a man of color
but as a human being
it becomes the only thing
so precious, that my ancestors
left to me
so, I shall honor it
walking and talking with
great pride
but also let them know
YOU DON"T OWN ME ANYMORE!!!

it feels like hate

when I enter a room and
your eyes don't look upon me
with LOVE
it feels like hate
when I stand to close to you
enough to hear your restless breath
it feels like hate
when I speak my mind, with loads
of pride
and then you roll your eyes
it feels like hate
I don't know you, never met you
but I'm really very easy
for you to despise
I know it in my heart and soul
that, it feels too much like hate

SWERVE

swerved

I shall NOT
be tricked again
believing your lies that
you want peace
I shall NOT be
fooled
into believing that YOU
really want
EQUALITY for all people
except for me
I shall NOT
be told that,
you want
RESPECT
but, never willing to give it
in return
I have been duped by
your anthems and
falsified fossilized amendments
that are only fit for those
who wrote it

7 shots

7 shots in the back,
isn't the kind of change
that came for a man
who's only crime was
just being black

the police weaponized Jacob Blake's rights
against him
they victimized his civil rights
as a human being
he never saw his life began to change
at the hands of those who were sworn
to serve and protect him
when will it stop, when will it end?
and the politicians still don't know when

he's chained to his bed, not even dead
and cant walk with his legs
so, when will this stop, when will this all end?
but nobody seems to know the answer
that is still blowing in the wind
or how to contain the vent up violence that is

still within them all as a culture that defines america
so where is the justice?
where is the respect as a human being that we need?
7 shots in the back is all you get,
for being black in a country full self righteous rage

down time

can we
just forget about
hating one another
because, it becomes more than just
about our color
can we, if only for today
just focus on love peace
and complete harmony
then come to a good understanding
between both you and me
can we?

selling out fast

your golden ticket will never last
and you're running out of time
Mr In-Between
because you are selling out fast
you can never hide who you really are
and what you claim to be
so if you want to belong

let us love

let us love
the people that sacrificed
their lives
who have died in vain for a
a better world to live in
let us love the people
who has shown us hate,
and they will all know
that we are all the same
let us remember all of those that have fallen
fighting for a cause worth dying for

death becomes us

in a country where an arrest results in
brutality and death
only in America, land of the free
home of the brave
it does
a routine traf ic stop becomes
the death sentence in my community
all over this country
at the hands of those with
a badge and gun
livin" in fear
as a black man entangled in
racial aggressions and prejudices
reliving those times we once knew
that we thought would never come again
but are now back with a vengeance
you will never feel protected or privileged
no matter your status in this society
because you are black
and that's all that really matters to
all of those who are putting that kind
of value on your life

front row

I sit here out on the battlefields
just like you
wearing my color
ready to fight for my life
so, if I should die, then so it shall be
there is no kind of living
without a democracy
I'm on the front row with my picket sign
in hand
marching for freedom,
taking a strong stand

my message to the black man

be prideful, bold and know
your place courteous and
kind in this society
make certain that you are firm in your beliefs
as a stranger in this foreign land
that owes you nothing but respect,
if you are willing to carry yourself with such grace
and class
be gracious courteous and kind
even to those who display racism
love all with true intentions and
never be concerned what's in it for you

in my world

in myworld
the cops shoots
a black man
before they could take
him to jail
in your world
the cops arrested
a white man and he
didn't catch any hell

in my world
racial tensions and
police brutality is
certainly on the rise,
"so ya better keep real close
my people"
Strength in Numbers,
if you want to survive

in my world
this is the most crucial time
to be alive
and if we don't all learn
from our history's past
then it will be our very own demise

all in

you wanted me dead, but not
before I challenge your authority
because your authority doesn't seem to
suit my kind
you wanted my life, but it's not
yours to sell anymore

KILLING FLOOR

killing floor

the whole world is
ready to attack
because they shot a black man
7 times in his back
no he didn't die, because it was in
God's will
and we'll keep on protesting and marching
hoping nobody else gets killed

racial tensions
and police brutality
is steadily on the rise
and we begin to see the hate building up
in those people's eyes
so, this becomes the most crucial time
to be alive

and if we don't learn from our history's past
then, it will certainly be our very own
demise

against the grain

how many more of us
must die,
in the name of Justice?
Freedom
is what we want
Equality
is what we need
not anymore
POLICE BRUTALITY

all they tell us is,
just be patient
you gotta believe
while being smothered with all
the prejudices
in this society,
until you just can't breathe

Black Lives Really Do Matter
so STAND UP!!!
against the injustices that
swallow you,
because they'll never let us
be FREE
protesting marching in the name of
Freedom
so, what else are we to do????

thirst for life

I thirst
for peace
harmony health
joy and all the other blessings
in life
it is the soul's sincerity
of my desires
I thirst for righteousness,
while the world is
in disarray
I thirst for knowledge,
while I am submerged beneath
a history that shows me
no fate

unknown

you used to be a
SUPERSTAR
but now you ain't nothin but
a burnt out unlit cigar
delusional and out of
your mind
and don't even realize that you
are completely behind in the times
Nobody , seems to know your name
because you killed your own dreams
and you are all the blame
I knew you, but
you don't remember me
so, who in the hell now
is gonna set you
FREE????

against the wall

if we can all just awaken
our minds,
there won't be as many of us still
dreaming.

you may call it JUSTICE Sir,
but, we call it how we see it,
how you show it and
how we feel it

thrown up against the wall
trying to, after over 400 yrs of oppression
discrimination and agitation
to show those people how to love
US

but, how can you love
if there is no Love
in your hearts

so, if we can all stay focused,
and keep ourselves
from falling into a somber sleep,
and hold the TRUTH to their faces,
well now,
wouldn't that be DEEP?

inside out

if my skin was pulled
inside out
would you have known
what color I was?
what ethnicity,
would you except me for who I am
not what I was?
would you love me like,
one of your own?
If you lost your sight,
would you know what my race is
even if I didn't acted or spoke like the black men
you thought you knew?
If my skin was pulled
inside out
would it really matter to you
of what kind of person I am?

suicide dreams

here lies
a man
not nearly Dead
committed self-inflicted
suicide dreams
not really quite sure
of what life means
down and out
loathing reality
but can he arise before it's too late,
or waste away on nothing but hate?
blaming the world for all the
choices he's made
something in life, has caused
his own fate
delusional fantasies corrupts his mind
for a cure that can only be
healed in time

freedom is mine

I am alone and solitarily confined
so i will never be free,
until freedom is mine
I want to I have to be free someday
and I hope that my freedom takes me
far far away

I would love to see sunny blue skies again
and on occasions the rain falling on my face
I would sacrifice one of my arms and a leg
if I could even take your place

I'm just here in this cell incarcerating
sitting around just killing time
and now I want freedom so bad
that I'm about to lose my mind

I want to be able to say out loud
hallelujah! hallelujah! I'm free at last...
free at last
and when I finally get paroled
I'd pray that I'll never have to come back

victimized

people in every city are
on the attack
because a cop shot a black man
7 times in his back
miraculously blessed that he's even survived
as people of color are left to wonder
the reasons why

but when will it end? where is the change?
as we all want to know,
will it always be the same?

I can't go here and they
won't let me go there,
and I'm prone to be killed by a cop
just about anywhere

so where is this justice?
where is the peace?
victimized everyday from police Brutality

being pulled over by a white cop could really be
very hazardous to your health
and you have a really good chance with that en-
counter
of it being a sentence of death

so when will it stop, when does this madness end?
I don't really know because, it's still somewhere
blowin' in the wind

war

this becomes a war
with so many casualties
people of color killed by the police
pursuing power in the name of the unjust
pointing a gun
with their shoot first and
ask questions later mentality
we need peace of mind in a time
of despair
in our age of less solidarity,
creativity and hope
let us all move beyond the politics
of our personal views and
righteousness beliefs
when is there a good time
to rise above it all?
take a chance on humanity

back to black

we been negroes
too long
we been colored
for so long
and African-Americans til then
but nigger, I been told they called us
for as long as we have been here
no changes no time for retreating
because Black is Back and we
are about to come into a crossroads of
time and prosperity
we are going old school, like the 60's
and much of the 70's
Back to Black, and we are not going
to turn back
from where we came and where
we are going
and we are no longer confined by the past
because, this is our future.

I refuse to breathe

Brutality has become the poetry
of our lives
Peace has become a song
they refuse to sing

Equality has no place in their hearts
and minds
with wanting Love becomes Hate

I thought I saw the young dying in the streets
but it was only an image from the past
that came in my dreams

I refuse to breathe
until the prejudices end, or die
a sudden agonizing death

I refuse to allow comfort to those who
refuse to let us live like we belong here

this is not their world, it belongs to us all
and until they see the error of their ways
we shall forever all be lost

power move

their power despises me
no hearts and love inside them
spending too much time
plotting against my own benefits

like the hypocrites they have become
they all live and die
with no souls

indiscretion

let's understand each other like
brothers and sisters
no race no color involved
just lovers.........of LIFE

let's treat each other like equals
brothers and sisters
the equivalence of GOD"S children
who like all others before us......we DREAM

tragedy

tragedy unfolds and no
dreams fulfilled
wasting one lifetime away
being unsure of many things

love becomes my first option
in these darkest times and
we remember not the days once lost
in time

love comes and goes
like a vengeful bitch leaving me
with memories left to ponder
that I care not to know
wasting one lifetime of love
is like dying a hundred deaths

but in the end, do you really care?

I camouflage my heart to protect it
from you all
then drift away on my own kind of love
my own kind of world

Roll Call

Slayed by the Beast

Gone but never forgotten

George Perry Floyd, October 14, 1973 - May 25, 2020
Powderhorn, Minneapolis, Minnesota
Knee on neck/Asphyxiated: May 25, 2020, Minneapolis Police Officer

Dreasjon "Sean" Reed, 1999 - May 6, 2020
Indianapolis, Indiana
Shot: May 6, 2020, Unidentified Indianapolis Metropolitan Police Officer

Michael Brent Charles Ramos, January 1, 1978 - April 24, 2020
Austin, Texas
Shot: April 24, 2020, Austin Police Detectives

Breonna Taylor, June 5, 1993 - March 13, 2020
Louisville, Kentucky
Shot: March 13, 2020, Louisville Metro Police Officers

Manuel "Mannie" Elijah Ellis, August 28, 1986 - March 3, 2020
Tacoma, Washington
Physical restraint/Hypoxia: March 3, 2020, Tacoma Police Officers

Atatiana Koquice Jefferson, November 28, 1990 - October 12, 2019
Fort Worth, Texas
Shot: October 12, 2019, Fort Worth Police Officer

Emantic "EJ" Fitzgerald Bradford Jr., June 18, 1997 - November 22, 2018
Hoover, Alabama
Shot: November 22, 2018, Unidentified Hoover Police Officers

Charles "Chop" Roundtree Jr., September 5, 2000 - October 17, 2018
San Antonio, Texas
Shot: October 17, 2018, San Antonio Police Officer

Chinedu Okobi, February 13, 1982 - October 3, 2018
Millbrae, California
Tasered/Electrocuted: October 3, 2018, San Mateo County Sherif Sergeant and Sheriff Deputies

Botham Shem Jean, September 29, 1991 - September 6, 2018
Dallas, Texas
Shot: September 6, 2018, Dallas Police Officer

Antwon Rose Jr., July 12, 2000 - June 19, 2018
East Pittsburgh, Pennsylvania
Shot: June 19, 2018, East Pittsburgh Police Officer

Saheed Vassell, December 22, 1983 - April 4, 2018
Brooklyn, New York City, New York
Shot: April 4, 2018, Four Unnamed New York City Police Officers

Stephon Alonzo Clark, August 10, 1995 – March 18, 2018
Sacramento, California
Shot: March 18, 2018, Sacramento Police Officers

Aaron Bailey, 1972 - June 29, 2017
Indianapolis, Indiana
Shot: June 29, 2017, Indianapolis Metropolitan Police Officers

Charleena Chavon Lyles, April 24, 1987 - June 18, 2017
Seattle, Washington
Shot: June 18, 2017, Seattle Police Officers

Fetus of Charleena Chavon Lyles (14-15 weeks), June 18, 2017
Seattle, Washington
Shot: June 18, 2017, Seattle Police Officers

Jordan Edwards, October 25, 2001 - April 29, 2017
Balch Springs, Texas
Shot: April 29, 2017, Balch Springs Officer

Chad Robertson, 1992 - February 15, 2017
Chicago, Illinois
Shot: February 8, 2017, Chicago Police Officer

Deborah Danner, September 25, 1950 - October 18, 2016
The Bronx, New York City, New York
Shot: October 18, 2016, New York City Police Officers

Alfred Olango, July 29, 1978 - September 27, 2016
El Cajon, California
Shot: September 27, 2016, El Cajon Police Officers

Terence Crutcher, August 16, 1976 - September 16, 2016
Tulsa, Oklahoma
Shot: September 16, 2016, Tulsa Police Officer

Terrence LeDell Sterling, July 31, 1985 - September 11, 2016
Washington, DC
Shot: September 11, 2016, Washington Metropolitan Police Officer

Korryn Gaines, August 24, 1993 - August 1, 2016
Randallstown, Maryland
Shot: August 1, 2016, Baltimore County Police

Joseph Curtis Mann, 1966 - July 11, 2016
Sacramento, California
Shot: July 11, 2016, Sacramento Police Officers

Philando Castile, July 16, 1983 - July 6, 2016
Falcon Heights, Minnesota
Shot: July 6, 2016, St. Anthony Police Officer

Alton Sterling, June 14, 1979 - July 5, 2016
Baton Rouge, Louisiana
Shot: July 5, 2016, Baton Rouge Police Officers

Bettie "Betty Boo" Jones, 1960 - December 26, 2015
Chicago, Illinois

Shot: December 26, 2015, Chicago Police Officer

Quintonio LeGrier, April 29, 1996 - December 26, 2015
Chicago, Illinois
Shot: December 26, 2015, Chicago Police Officer

Corey Lamar Jones, February 3, 1984 - October 18, 2015
Palm Beach Gardens, Florida
Shot: October 18, 2015, Palm Beach Gardens Police Officer

Jamar O'Neal Clark, May 3, 1991 - November 16 2015
Minneapolis, Minnesota
Shot: November 15, 2015, Minneapolis Police Officers

Jeremy "Bam Bam" McDole, 1987 - September 23, 2015
Wilmington, Delaware
Shot: September 23, 2015, Wilmington Police Officers

India Kager, June 9, 1988 - September 5, 2015
Virginia Beach, Virginia
Shot: September 5, 2015, Virginia Beach Police Officers

Samuel Vincent DuBose, March 12, 1972 - July 19, 2015
Cincinnati, Ohio
Shot: July 19, 2015, University of Cincinnati Police Officer

Sandra Bland, February 7, 1987 - July 13, 2015
Waller County, Texas
Excessive Force/Wrongful Death/Suicide (?): July 10, 2015, Texas State Trooper

Brendon K. Glenn, 1986 - May 5, 2015
Venice, California
Shot: May 5, 2015, Los Angeles Police Officer

Freddie Carlos Gray Jr., August 16, 1989 – April 19, 2015
Baltimore, Maryland
Brute Force/Spinal Injuries: April 12, 2015, Baltimore City Police Officers

Walter Lamar Scott, February 9, 1965 - April 4, 2015
North Charleston, South Carolina

Shot: April 4, 2015, North Charleston Police Officer

Eric Courtney Harris, October 10, 1971 - April 2, 2015
Tulsa, Oklahoma
Shot: April 2, 2015, Tulsa County Reserve Deputy

Phillip Gregory White, 1982 - March 31, 2015
Vineland, New Jersey
K-9 Mauling/Respiratory distress: March 31, 2015, Vineland Police Officers

Mya Shawatza Hall, December 5, 1987 – March 30, 2015
Fort Meade, Maryland
Shot: March 30, 2015, National Security Agency Police Officers

Meagan Hockaday, August 27, 1988 - March 28, 2015
Oxnard, California
Shot: March 28, 2015, Oxnard Police Officer

Tony Terrell Robinson, Jr., October 18, 1995 - March 6, 2015
Madison, Wisconsin
Shot: March 6, 2015, Madison Police Officer

Janisha Fonville, March 3, 1994 - February 18, 2015
Charlotte, North Carolina
Shot: February 18, 2015, Charlotte-Mecklenburg Police Officer

Natasha McKenna, January 9, 1978 - February 8, 2015
Fairfax County, Virginia
Tasered/Cardiac Arrest: February 3, 2015, Fairfax County Sheriff Deputies

Jerame C. Reid, June 8, 1978 - December 30, 2014
Bridgeton, New Jersey
Shot: December 30, 2014, Bridgeton Police Officer

Rumain Brisbon, November 24, 1980 – December 2, 2014
Phoenix, Arizona
Shot: December 2, 2014, Phoenix Police Officer

Tamir Rice, June 15, 2002 - November 22, 2014

Cleveland, Ohio
Shot: November 22, 2014, Cleveland Police Officer

Akai Kareem Gurley, November 12, 1986 - November 20, 2014
Brooklyn, New York City, New York
Shot: November 20, 2014, New York City Police Officer

Tanisha N. Anderson, January 22, 1977 - November 13, 2014
Cleveland, Ohio
Physically Restrained/Brute Force: November 13, 2014, Cleveland Police Officers

Dante Parker, August 14, 1977 - August 12, 2014
Victorville, California
Tasered/Excessive Force: August 12, 2014, San Bernardino County Sheriff Deputies

Ezell Ford, October 14, 1988 - August 11, 2014
Florence, Los Angeles, California
Shot: August 11, 2014, Los Angeles Police Officers

Michael Brown Jr., May 20, 1996 - August 9, 2014
Ferguson, Missouri
Shot: August 9, 2014, Ferguson Police Officer

John Crawford III, July 29, 1992 - August 5, 2014
Beavercreek, Ohio
Shot: August 5, 2014, Beavercreek Police Officer

Eric Garner, September 15, 1970 - July 17, 2014
Staten Island, New York
Choke hold/Suffocated: July 17, 2014, New York City Police Officer

Dontre Hamilton, January 20, 1983 - April 30, 2014
Milwaukee, Wisconsin
Shot: April 30, 2014, Milwaukee Police Officer

Victor White III, September 11, 1991 - March 3, 2014
New Iberia, Louisiana
Shot: March 2, 2014, Iberia Parish Sheriff Deputy

Gabriella Monique Nevarez, November 25, 1991 - March 2, 2014

Citrus Heights, California
Shot: March 2, 2014, Citrus Heights Police Officers

Yvette Smith, December 18, 1966 - February 16, 2014
Bastrop County, Texas
Shot: February 16, 2014, Bastrop County Sheriff Deputy

McKenzie J. Cochran, August 25, 1988 – January 29, 2014
Southfield, Michigan
Pepper Sprayed/Compression Asphyxiation: January 28, 2014, Northland Mall Security Guards

Jordan Baker, 1988 - January 16, 2014
Houston, Texas
Shot: January 16, 2014, Off-duty Houston Police Officer

Andy Lopez, June 2, 2000 - October 22, 2013
Santa Rosa, California
Shot: October 22, 2013, Sonoma County Sheriff Deputy

Miriam Iris Carey, August 12, 1979 - October 3, 2013
Washington, DC
Shot 26 times: October 3, 2013, U. S. Secret Service Officer

Barrington "BJ" Williams, 1988 - September 17, 2013
New York City, New York
Neglect/Disdain/Asthma Attack: September 17, 2013, New York City Police Officers

Jonathan Ferrell, October 11, 1989 - September 14, 2013
Charlotte, North Carolina
Shot: September 14, 2013, Charlotte-Mecklenburg Police Officer

Carlos Alcis, 1970 - August 15, 2013
Brooklyn, New York City
Heart Attack/Neglect: August 15, 2013, New York City Police Officers

Larry Eugene Jackson Jr., November 29, 1980 - July 26, 2013
Austin, Texas
Shot: July 26, 2013, Austin Police Detective

Kyam Livingston, July 29, 1975 - July 21, 2013

New York City, New York
Neglect/Ignored pleas for help: July 20-21, 2013, New York City Police Officers

Clinton R. Allen, September 26, 1987 - March 10, 2013
Dallas, Texas
Tasered and Shot: March 10, 2013, Dallas Police Officer

Kimani "KiKi" Gray, October 19, 1996 - March 9, 2013
Brooklyn, New York City, New York
Shot: March 9, 2013, New York Police Officers

Kayla Moore, April 17, 1971 - February 13, 2013
Berkeley, California
Restrained face-down prone: February 12, 2013, Berkeley Police Officers

Jamaal Moore Sr., 1989 - December 15, 2012
Chicago, Illinois
Shot: December 15, 2012, Chicago Police Officer

Johnnie Kamahi Warren, February 26, 1968 - February 13, 2012
Dothan, Alabama
Tasered/Electrocuted: December 10, 2012, Houston County (AL) Sheriff Deputy

Shelly Marie Frey, April 21, 1985 - December 6, 2012
Houston, Texas
Shot: December 6, 2012, Off-duty Harris County Sheriff's Deputy

Darnisha Diana Harris, December 11, 1996 - December 2, 2012
Breaux Bridge, Louisiana
Shot: December 2, 2012, Breaux Bridge Police Offfice

Timothy Russell, December 9. 1968 - November 29, 2012
Cleveland, Ohio
137 Rounds/Shot 23 times: November 29, 2012, Cleveland Police Officers

Malissa Williams, June 20, 1982 - November 29, 2012
Cleveland, Ohio

137 Rounds/Shot 24 times: November 29, 2012, Cleveland Police Officers

Noel Palanco, November 28, 1989 - October 4, 2012
Queens, New York City, New York
Shot: October 4, 2012, New York City Police Officers

Reynaldo Cuevas, January 6, 1992 - September 7, 2012
Bronx, New York City, New York
Shot: September 7, 2012, New York City Police Officer

Chavis Carter, 1991 - July 28, 2012
Jonesboro, Arkansas
Shot: July 28, 2012, Jonesboro Police Officer

Alesia Thomas, June 1, 1977 - July 22, 2012
Los Angeles, California
Brutal Force/Beaten: July 22, 2012, Los Angeles Police Officers

Shantel Davis, May 26, 1989 - June 14, 2012
New York City, New York
Shot: June 14, 2012, New York City Police Officer

Sharmel T. Edwards, October 10, 1962 - April 21, 2012
Las Vegas, Nevada
Shot: April 21, 2012, Las Vegas Police Officers

Tamon Robinson, December 21, 1985 - April 18, 2012
Brooklyn, New York City, New York
Run over by police car: April 12, 2012, New York City Police Officers

Ervin Lee Jefferson, III, 1994 - March 24, 2012
Atlanta, Georgia
Shot: March 24, 2012, Shepperson Security & Escort Services Security Guards

Kendrec McDade, May 5, 1992 - March 24, 2012
Pasadena, California
Shot: March 24, 2012, Pasadena Police Officers

Rekia Boyd, November 5, 1989 - March 21, 2012
Chicago, Illinois

Shot: March 21, 2012, Off-duty Chicago Police Detective

Shereese Francis, 1982 - March 15, 2012
Queens, New York City, New York
Suffocated to death: March 15, 2012, New York City Police Officers

Jersey K. Green, June 17, 1974 - March 12, 2012
Aurora, Illinois
Tasered/Electrocuted: March 12, 2012, Aurora Police Officers

Wendell James Allen, December 19, 1991 – March 7, 2012
New Orleans, Louisiana
Shot: March 7, 2012, New Orleans Police Officer

Nehemiah Lazar Dillard, July 29, 1982 - March 5, 2012
Gainesville, Florida
Tasered/Electrocuted: March 5, 2012, Alachua County Sheriff Deputies

Dante' Lamar Price, July 18, 1986 - March 1, 2012
Dayton, Ohio
Shot: March 1, 2012, Ranger Security Guards

Raymond Luther Allen Jr., 1978 - February 29, 2012
Galveston, Texas
Tasered/Electrocuted: February 27, 2012, Galveston Police Officers

Manual Levi Loggins Jr., February 22, 1980 - February 7, 2012
San Clemente, Orange County, California
Shot: February 7, 2012, Orange County Sheriff Deputy

Ramarley Graham, April 12, 1993 - February 2, 2012
The Bronx, New York City, New York
Shot: February 2, 2012, New York City Police Officer

Kenneth Chamberlain Sr., April 12, 1943 - November 19, 2011
White Plains, New York
Tasered/Electrocuted/Shot: November 19, 2011, White Plains Police Officers

Alonzo Ashley, June 10, 1982 - July 18, 2011
Denver, Colorado

Tasered/Electrocuted: July 18, 2011, Denver Police Officers

Derek Williams, January 23, 1989 - July 6, 2011
Milwaukee, Wisconsin
Blunt Force/Respiratory distress: July 6, 2011, Milwaukee Police Officers

Raheim Brown, Jr., March 4, 1990 - January 22, 2011
Oakland, California
Shot: January 22, 2011, Oakland Unified School District Police

Reginald Doucet, June 3, 1985 - January 14, 2011
Los Angeles, California
Shot: January 14, 2011, Los Angeles Police Officer

Derrick Jones, September 30, 1973 - November 8, 2010
Oakland, California
Shot: November 8, 2010, Oakland Police Officers

Danroy "DJ" Henry Jr., October 29, 1990 - October 17, 2010
Pleasantville, New York
Shot: October 17, 2020, Pleasantville Police Officer

Aiyana Mo'Nay Stanley-Jones, July 20, 2002 - May 16, 2010
Detroit, Michigan
Shot: May 16, 2010, Detroit Police Officer

Steven Eugene Washington, September 20, 1982 - March 20, 2010
Los Angeles, California
Shot: March 20, 2010, Los Angeles County Police

Aaron Campbell, September 7, 1984 - January 29, 2010
Portland, Oregon
Shot: January 29, 2010, Portland Police Officer

Kiwane Carrington, July 14, 1994 - October 9, 2009
Champaign, Illinois
Shot: October 9, 2019, Champaign Police Officer

Victor Steen, November 11, 1991 - October 3, 2009
Pensacola, Florida
Tasered/Run over: October 3, 2009, Pensacola Police Officer

Shem Walker, March 18, 1960 - July 11, 2009
Brooklyn, New York
Shot: July 11, 2009, New York City Undercover C94 Police Officer

Oscar Grant III, February 27, 1986 - January 1, 2009
Oakland, California
Shot: January 1, 2009, BART Police Officer

Tarika Wilson, October 30, 1981 - January 4, 2008
Lima, Ohio
Shot January 4, 2008, Lima Police Officer

DeAunta Terrel Farrow, September 7, 1994 – June 22, 2007
West Memphis, Arkansas
Shot: June 22, 2007, West Memphis (AR) Police Officer

Sean Bell, May 23, 1983 - November 25, 2006
Queens, New York City, New York
Shot: November 25, 2006, New York City Police Officers

Kathryn Johnston, June 26, 1914 - November 21, 2006
Atlanta, Georgia
Shot: November 21, 2006, Undercover Atlanta Po lice Officers

Ronald Curtis Madison, March 1, 1965 - September 4, 2005
Danziger Bridge, New Orleans, Louisiana
Shot: September 4, 2005, New Orleans Police Officers

James B. Brissette Jr., November 6, 1987 - September 4, 2005
Danziger Bridge, New Orleans, Louisiana
Shot: September 4, 2005, New Orleans Police Officers

Henry "Ace" Glover, October 2, 1973 - September 2, 2005
New Orleans, Louisiana
Shot: September 2, 2005, New Orleans Police Officers

Timothy Stansbury, Jr., November 16, 1984 - January 24, 2004
Brooklyn, New York City, New York
Shot: January 24, 2004, New York City Police Officer

Ousmane Zongo, 1960 - May 22, 2003
New York City, New York

Shot: May 22, 2003, New York City Police Officer

Alberta Spruill, 1946 - May 16, 2003
New York City, New York
Stun grenade thrown into her apartment led to a heart attack: May 16, 2003, New York City Police Officer

Kendra Sarie James, December 24, 1981 - May 5, 2003
Portland, Oregon
Shot: May 5, 2003, Portland Police Officer

Orlando Barlow, December 29, 1974 – February 28, 2003
Las Vegas, Nevada
Shot: February 28, 2003, Las Vegas Police Officer

Timothy DeWayne Thomas Jr., July 25, 1981 - April 7, 2001
Cincinnati, Ohio
Shot: April 7, 2001, Cincinnati Police Patrolman

Ronald Beasley, 1964 - June 12, 2000
Dellwood, Missouri
Shot: June 12, 2000, Dellwood Police Officers

Earl Murray, 1964 - June 12, 2000
Dellwood, Missouri
Shot: June 12, 2000, Dellwood Police Officers

Patrick Moses Dorismond, February 28, 1974 - March 16, 2000
New York City, New York
Shot: March 16, 2000, New York City Police Officer

Prince Carmen Jones Jr., March 30, 1975 - September 1, 2000
Fairfax County, Virginia
Shot: September 1, 2000, Prince George's County Police Officer

Malcolm Ferguson, October 31, 1976 - March 1, 2000
The Bronx, New York City, New York
Shot: March 1, 2000, New York City Police Officer

LaTanya Haggerty, 1973 - June 4, 1999
Chicago, Illinois
Shot: June 4, 1999, Chicago Police Officer

Margaret LaVerne Mitchell, 1945 - May 21, 1999
Los Angeles, California
Shot: May 21, 1999, Los Angeles Police Officer

Amadou Diallo, September 2, 1975 - February 4, 1999
The Bronx, New York City, New York
Shot: February 4, 1999, New York City Police Officers

Tyisha Shenee Miller, March 9, 1979 – December 28, 1998
Riverside, California
Shot: December 28, 1998, Riverside Police Officers

Dannette Daniels, January 25, 1966 - June 7, 1997
Newark, New Jersey
Shot: June 7, 1997, Newark Police Officer

Frankie Ann Perkins, 1960 - March 22, 1997
Chicago, Illinois
Brutal Force/Strangled: March 22, 1997, Chicago Police Officers

Nicholas Heyward Jr., August 26, 1981 - September 27, 1994
Brooklyn, New York City, New York
Shot: September 27, 1994, New York City Police Officer

Mary Mitchell, 1950 - November 3, 1991
The Bronx, New York City, New York
Shot: November 3, 1991, New York City Police Officer

Yvonne Smallwood, 1959 - December 9, 1987
New York City, New York
Severely beaten/Massive blood clot: December 3, New York City Police Officers

Eleanor Bumpers, August 22, 1918 - October 29, 1984
The Bronx, New York City, New York
Shot: October 29, 1984, New York City Police Officer

Michael Jerome Stewart, May 9, 1958 – September 28, 1983
New York City, New York
Brutal Force: September 15, 1983, New York City Transit Police

Eula Mae Love, August 8, 1939 - January 3, 1979

Los Angeles, California
Shot: January 3, 1979, Los Angeles County Police Officers

Arthur Miller Jr., 1943 - June 14, 1978
Brooklyn, New York City, New York
Chokehold/Strangled: June 14, 1978, New York City Police Officers

Randolph Evans, April 5, 1961 - November 25, 1976
Brooklyn, New York City, New York
Shot in head: November 25, 1976, New York City Police Officer

Barry Gene Evans, August 29, 1958 - February 10, 1976
Los Angeles, California
Shot: February 10, 1976, Los Angeles Police Officers

Rita Lloyd, January 27, 1973
New York City, New York
Shot: January 27, 1973, New York City Police Officer

Henry Dumas, July 20, 1934 - May 23, 1968
Harlem, New York City, New York
Shot: May 23, 1968, New York City Transit Police Officer

About The Author

H.E.Edwards is the author of "Essence of Soul" love poems and "Tao of Blackness" Volume 1 as well as a musician and indie artist who was born and raised in Houston, Texas. He began writing poetry over two decades ago and some of his works was

featured in the early issues of Urban Beat magazine and several other poetry anthologies. He has also won several awards for his poetry throughout his writing career. H.E.Edwards gets his inspiration from poetry greats such as Sandra Cisneros, Rudyard Kipling, Edgar Allen Poe, Emily Dickinson, Rita Dove, Nikki Giovanni,Paul Laurence Dunbar, Amiri Baraka and William Shakespeare. He now lives in his native city Houston with his family where he enjoys writing and working on his own music.

Contact and Social Media:

Email: heedwardspoems@gmail.com

Twitter: @heedwardspoetry

Instagram: @heedwardspoetry1